MAYALAND

MAYALAND

John Moritz

First Intensity Press
Lawrence, Kansas

Acknowledgment: I wish to thank the editors of the following publications in which some of these poems, often a variation on the present form, first appeared: *Skanky Possum* (Dale Smith and Hoa Nguyen), *House Organ* (Kenneth Warren), *First Intensity* (Lee Chapman). Some of these poems were also published in a chapbook: *Mayaland: 8 poems, 2 essays* by Jim McCrary and John Moritz.

Cover colorist: Jessica Kolokol
Book design: First Intensity Book Arts
www.FirstIntensity.com

Published by
First Intensity Press
P.O. Box 665
Lawrence, KS 66044

The Monkey Scribes appear in the great epic, Popol Vuh, which was written in Latin, 16th c., by a literate Quiche Maya who transcribed the work from glyphs shortly after conquest. In the late 17th c. Father Francisco Ximenez copied and translated the earlier document. Since then both the Latin and glyphs have been lost.

The Monkey Scribes were the Hero Twins' brothers (Mayans loved duality) and they constantly complained to their grandmother that the Hero Twins weren't pulling their weight in the fields. At some point the Hero Twins had enough of their brothers' whining and transformed them into the Monkey Scribes so that their exploits with the Lords of the Underworld would be recorded.

Señor Chavez, manager at Hertz, drove us to the airport. As a child he had gone to Dzibilchatun, long before restoration, for family picnics. He had also been a jarara dancer balancing a tray with many bottles of beer on his head at a restaurant in Chichen-Itza. He asked the inevitable, "How did you like your stay in the Yucatan?"

"Too much carnival, no, not carnival, Disneyland."

He leaned back and laughed. "No, not Disneyland, Mayaland!"

Dzibilchaltun

Windows are a Maya rarity all to ourselves
at the Temple of the Seven Dolls, so labeled for what
the dirt diggers, wearing sweaty henniquin panamas
unearthed with an attitude straight in the face
of the air conditioned code crackers
seven little clay stick figures, each with its own
particular deformity, excavated from the serpent's chamber
beneath our cerebral hammock-slung morning
less complicated mistaking the THING for silence
while I scan the alien runway which leads to the market
and the late 16th c. Spanish barrel vault built by ruin stone
to the she of the cenote who backstrokes
in cool waters to impress her boyfriends
who sit on the ledge chatting and smoking Marlboros
she's the big crab, the fish laugh
from the bottom of the pool

Ruta Maya Unravel Our Heads in the Yucatan

arrived at five in Merida
        checked in at the Gran
where journalist Alma Reed stayed
when she blew the whistle on Edward Thompson
and the Peabody gang's looting Chichen-Itza
via diplomatic pouch,
Castro also a guest, as was Porfirio Diaz
another cold hearted mother killer
masterbated in his room fantasizing
Paseo de Montejo   Merida's Champs Élysées
.but this afternoon the Gran celeb
is Rico, big Lab stretched
out on the floor, tail slapping the tile
glad to be alive, as Cream

Orchids grow in the lobby more courtyard than lobby
palms reach for the sun from a bear-claw bathtub

                    At the Parque Hidalgo
          piñãtas swing
                    and strands
          and strands
                    of colored lights
          hang above
                    a mirimba band
          which seemingly
                    plays
          the same tune over
                    and over

so to close this night, why not
from a manuscript
                    1566, quoting an early
horse invader, Friar Diego de Landa, proto mother killer
Franciscan book burning historian
who was even too much for the Inquisition
called back to Spain

> "I, Diego de Landa, say I saw a great tree near the village
> upon the branches of which a captain had hung many women,
> with their infant children hung from their feet. At this town
> and nother two leagues away called Verey they hung two
> women, one a maiden, the other recently married, for no other
> crime than their beauty, and because of fearing a disturbance
> among the soldiers on their account; also further to cause the
> Indians to believe the Spaniards indifferent to their women.
> The memory of these two is kept both among the Indians and
> Spaniards on account of their great beauty and the cruelty
> with which they were killed."

ACQUITTED!
                    While vendors sell
                    oranges dipped in habañero dust

Thursday nights belong to the park
Santa Lucia, a few blocks up
from the austere Jesuit
Temple of Jesus, 17th c. vaulted ceiling
centuries of grime and stain
                   built not long before
Rome said, Jesuits, pack your bags
a buffer from the jam of
traffic and police whistles

high heels and tight skirts high heels
embroidered jackets, Anne Waldman scarves
John Lee Hooker's spin and
groove in the mind's Wurlitzer
their men strut, black slacks, guayaberas,
jackets or vests, bandanas tied at the neck
their men are cool, their men are reptiles
          the few Maya in the crowd have a delicate
          crushed beauty all their own
On stage an old man, impeccably
tells a tale of spider-monkeys climbing ruins
his forefathers built, tonight they celebrate
"30 anos de la tradicional seranata Yucateca"
particularly Luis Sabina, the agency's head culture
vulture since its inception, honored
by the police band striking up a few of his compositions
Lines set to a *bolero:*

          "I wish with all my life, what this remote injustice is, to make
          sense of this suffering, and what in every night is an absence,
          only pain and confusion increases my passion."

not bad for a two-day, as Olson said, a shit tourist town

CHICHEN

13 Friday   T   5a.   dawn, smoked a cigarette outside our room,
up those   Z   vast   watching staff on the rooftop pour water
moments   A   before from gallon jugs onto palms in the court-
                        yard below.

        Chichen-Itza . . .   Hot and humid!

gate opened at the court of a thousand columns
El Castillo to our west
the Toltecs achieved what they wanted
intimidation, used the sharpest flint off the shelf
constructing their city over
existing structures, to awe and impress

they were the conquerors
obstinate, and
insecure, this was a city
where warriors
were equal to priests
brought with them
Kukulcan, green feathered
serpent genius

unlike the Itzas
they were respected

warrior columns support nothing
but to enhance the sense of a military formation
portraits etched in stone
leading to Chacmool, I climbed for the rub and view
the narrow steps, purposely so

in order to facilitate the removal of a heartless corpse
at the top I was quite hot and out of breath
reaching into my pocket for a cigarette

"Hey Chac, what do you think about
all these beaters out on the plaza?"
No, I did not rub the bowl which received the hearts
there was an indolence to this
turtle head with a smirk, reclined
lording *it* over the plain, I did not want to get familiar with
so we kept a social distance while I smoked

SHE WAS A VENUS PLATFORM DANCER

> ". . . where they say farces were presented and comedies
> for the public." — Friar de Landa, 1566

She was a Venus platform dancer
on her left shoulder was a tattoo of the moon
on the right the sun, her flesh was ample enough
to bare all the planets between
she danced over Chac's tomb
she was part of the terminal scene
She was a Venus platform dancer
and could predict an eclipse but not say where
and learned her stagecraft
from the hero twins, she was Maya duality
big ass leg burner-head gobbling dart thrower
she had bounce to perfection
she could sever a heart or impale
a skull with her tongue
She was a Venus platform dancer

LA SONIDA Y LUZ

Chichen-Itza 18 January '99

Sitting in a folding chair on the plaza
warm night, sound and light
along with Mayaland busload casualties wheeled in
from Cancun, sunblock and cameras, stepping all over the ruins
rubbing the Jaguar for the album
while jarana dancers dance
again, the night is warm
                        light diversion
while the sound has a loudspeaker anthro-distortion
equal to the Itzas who spoke Maya badly
and farted in public . . . asi que pasa?

out of a watery chaos, null and
void, an endless sea, without beginning
without history, the ancient gods, Tepeu and
Gucumatz fashioned the earth and
grew bored. These divine generators
realized plants and animals were not enough
to venerate their ingenuity

lean back to another Mayaland behind the thin veneer
of agency, buses and hotels
                                        N
                                        O

Mayaland where the light is green   A
                                    B on the Venus platform dancers
who choose to cant their tilt on a line, R
                                    A   *no abrazos while I kiss the sky*
                                    Z   *in my no abrazos mind*
Experience is the first chime   O   as such, wisdom and dream
are shade for those who dance   S   over the rain god, old
Chac's tomb, lean back
from the rubble chorus

   Enter: Kukulcan coiled like a wedding cake
                                    Gucumatz to the Quiche
Popol Vuh, reptilian in the absolute
So the Gods sat back.
             3:44 PM slithering down the steps of El Castillo
and the platform dancers place
quetzal feathers in their hair

        So they shaped proto creatures from mud but
        all too soon to mud returned. A race of stick figures
        were next to make the scene but
        these manikins couldn't even keep a beat and
        were torched, only to be replaced by men and
        women made from flesh who had the rhythm but
        were carnal and virulent.

             when the 2nd set of Hero Twins arrive
at the ball court for the court at Chichen-Itza is worthy
of the Twins since there is no longer a place
to view Quiche, torn from the world
they arrive nameless and undescribed to the Lords
of the Underworld

        The game might play something like this
        checking out the dawn from a blowgun
        Hunahpu's head is snatched by a bat
        some say turtle   others pumpkin shell   or squash
        possum fashioned   replaces the brother's head

        rabbit on a take-off roll runs with the ball
        off court distracting the Lords
        while little Balanque lifts his brother's head
        from the Lords' trophy shelf
        then squash becomes the ball thrown out onto the court
                                squash worn with memory
        so when punted duality bursts open upon a field
                                within the zodiac
        a spate of seeds releases the being
        dawn opens her mouth to
        wait for Venus and the sun will follow

        the Twins knew the game was theirs
        the Lords, defeated, hadn't a clue

On this night a trashed-out satellite clicks through Pleiades
known as the 400 Boys, more accurate than the Greek
where once copal burned, tonight smoke rises from Marlboros
La Luz, the light show also clicks

pastels flash back and forth
from Jaguar to Chacmool
while loudspeakers inform
Toltecs invaded from the sea
"on a raft of serpents" we flew over at 27,000 ft
on wings Guatemala drinking a glass
of Chardonnay, while I read Michael Coe's *The Maya*
for the gossip about the grim exiles from the West

> *These forefather gods anxious for*
> *praise called for a black rain*
> *to flood the earth and annihilate them all.*

One death and Seven summon the boys to the palace
once again the Twins arrive undescribed, nameless
and cautious, urchins who never knew their father
who speak to the Lords with eyes cast down
Dance!
      the tramps oblige

knew a bandstand girl who could trot to the Armadillo
and did the Weasel by a lake once but only the boys
could dance on stilts to the goatsucker blues

Dance and kill the dog!
                One death and Seven bark
      the tramps oblige
Set the house on fire!
      the tramps oblige

and return the dog to life
wagging his tail, as glad as Cream

when flame and smoke subside
                            nothing is charred

One death and Seven are impressed
as Road kill and Pus dread are
as Filthy demon is

                for the Twins know their metaphors
how to *describe* the rude and slack
they know what confusion a pun can do
they know all the possibilities of rhyme
they are a walking footnote

hallucinogenic enemas administered
by the unfortunate daughters of Lust woman
arouse the Lords to a frenzy

Do yourselves with an obsidian blade!
so little Balanque dances alone
Hanahpu's head rolls, his heart wrapped in a leaf
hey bro, get it together
which he does
again the Twins are dancing

We've got the frenzy, Do us!
no problem, the kids reply
            this should be as easy
            as a punch line
One death and Seven are butchered
but their limbs and heads, their hearts remain on the floor
the lesser lords get the message
split through the back door leading to the road

but there is no escape

> *Tepeu and Gucumatz, who created the earth*
> *endowed it with plants and animals, started*
> *all over again. This time kayem, corn dough,*
> *was kneaded and believers*
> *walked the earth to do their bidding and*
> *the gods sat back.*

Now we will tell you our names;
I am Hanahpu   I am Balanque
here to avenge our father, you remember our fathers
you are no more than Owl, than the stinking Itza
you will be lost in translation   the ball game is over

their father appears   their fathers appear
I was a head hung from a tree when I spat on your mother's palm
Farewell!   And the Hero Twins ascend
to the heart of heaven
we know as Sun and Venus

pull the plug on the loudspeakers
there is nothing more to say after the Itza
pastels dim by conquest

Leaving Piste

Barking dogs, carnal pits
muscle behind the restoration
goodbye Chichen-Itza
to seek out how you bury your dead
driving north to Merida
soul worms follow a path of marigolds
to celebrate la familia
cemetery town with slab and cross
or pyramid, pitched roofs
like the villages with a square and festival

       grow
more prosperous closer
    to the *white city*

yet the unkept, where the gate was locked
watching the young boy
who dropped the soccer ball
to keep an eye on the gringos, stood hand to hip
then kicked it up for a bounce and bounce
elbow to head to knee
showing off like the Twins at the ballcourt,

       is what there is

CHACMULTUN

So what! or why?   to come to this, The Distance
for red stone, and rubble core, dirt road village
dogs claim, and pigs wallow, dirt road game cock struts across
with emblazoned hackles the last to celebrate
for there's already a fresh hostility
along with a coca-cola sign and a generator
too many roads, too few places before the Caterpillar
clears the jungle, numbers stones
and from a world away to view the banded columns
and not to step on any of that *shit*

an iguana startled by yet another Alien
since the high Puuc mosaic
rushes for cover, limestone absorbs the terror
alone among the ruins, what Olson feared
who would be there to suck out a reptile's poison

And the fear is a mesozoic rush
straight from Bolio's *Rattlesnake School*
for the Maya believed themselves to be
the aggressive Ahua Can
and flattened their foreheads
adorned themselves with snake tattoos
lined their teeth with geometric patterns
resembling the skin or rattles
quetzal feathers and scales for the solar shaker

I learned from Francis Parkman what he learned
                              slowly at the Sioux camp
        drop the baggage   eat the dog   don't trespass

        with enough Maya to fill a Marlboro pack
        Spanish for a carton, brings a morning lost in thicket
        when Sharon and I came upon a simple
        stone dwelling, thatched roof, no windows, two doorways
        allow for a breeze, a hammock slung inside,
        I asked the man of this place,
        "El camino," guidebook Spanish, "donde esta?"
        he answered in Mayan, to let me know *exactly where I was*
        then Spanish and by gestures directed us to the highway.
        Remembering an occasion from *The Shoshoneans*
        I offered him a pack of Marlboros.
                              He too was overjoyed.
Tobacco is very complicated
                    and should never have been allowed
to be casual like a habit.

CALL ME UXMAL!

said the Dwarf
for I hatched
from a reptile egg

because an old woman
whose house

        had rags
and a corner

        nourished
and chided me

I call her mother
because of her

I built this house, my house
the House of the Dwarf

my skull withstood the challenge of stones
I wear the tortilla crown
not the Governor

my mother died proud

*　*　*

Whittled from an account

                              John Lloyd Stephens heard

while sitting in the corbel arch

                              at the Governors

from a woman relegated
      to making tortillas
for the young boy hired on
as translator was a better cook
      Maya lips to Stephens' ear
      while his eyes observed
      the pyramid at dusk

one journey
etched into the next

         We too were there
where the Dwarf bathes at sunset

in a limestone patchwork so close, I dare not speak of
the touch of capability dragged to this spot where stones move
for only a moment, until we blink, we're staring into the flower
of the cosmos, rid of the noise

but near Mani there is a cave where an old woman sits
in the shade of a large tree and trades clear water
from the cenote for a mother's criatura
who she feeds to the serpent beside her
the old woman is said to be the mother of the Dwarf

KABAH

Is a drive thru
terminal cheese
straddling 261
done w/ an arch
and the codz-poop chac gross
indicates to the dirt diggers
that the puuc hill Maya
may have had a factory scene
churning out these masks
w/ Olsonic curled *phallus*
true proportions
rain catchers, O gee
in the big snake's hand
on the origin road

but the morning sun wasn't too warm
and you couldn't miss it
just when the map blew out the window
we threw the hopper in reverse
because the palace looked cool
w/ its roof comb top
stopped and lingered till noon

CELESTUN

at the road block the Captain asks what we're smuggling
but I thought he wants to know
what we're doing in Celestun
so I say, "Aqui mirar a los flamingos
"

well, that's when he orders
a very young boy with an automatic
to raise the hood on the VW
we call jungle hopper, and there's only the spare
which the boy stares at for a moment
then thumps it hard with his very young fist

what was that all about? you ask

I surmise with an eye in the rear view
we're the burger between the buns
this road traffics everything from
mushrooms to organs, reefer to guns
where the green-Gos.
I surmise by this route it's logical
Thompson hauled off stones from the Zone Archeological
yes, this road has had its run
since the horse bore the Spaniards
I've been told that gold to the Maya
was excrement from the sun

and we laughed carefully breaking down the spare
taking hold of the plumed serpent
who emerged from the tire with only a single bruise

BULLET HOLES, YELLOW WALLS

Never marry your mistress
as Governor Carillo Puerto
desired gold on Alma Reed's finger
she in New York typing her notes
for an exposé on Edward Thompson
and the Peabody gang's
pillage of Chichen-Itza
for the *Times*

heat lightning is intense tonight
from the Gran balcony
toward the north over Progresso
and a pier bound for Houston
various outlines "with the redness of the sky"
and the indiscretions by the clouds in Carillo's gulf

writing his proclamation for land reform
couldn't let the ink dry on the vellum
before tacking on a decree to legalize divorce
during the henniquin boom
brought in the Lebanese trade
and the raw, bloody hands of
Castro Pacheco's painting
was all Rome
and the hacienda lords needed
to have Carillo taken out and shot

A song was written about it
so romantica from heart to sleeve
only a button could halt
"the flowers of perfumed nectars"
but the one I heard
just down the street
                    "Love Stinks"

BIG SCREEN rolls off as we enter. Nebraska lost to Missouri. A funk band from Kansas City, pg 2, is scheduled to perform after the game. The pool chalker directs us to a booth beyond his stick. Pg 2 is a racial mix: trombone and sax are white, bass, rhythm guitars and drums are black. The crowd is mostly falling down not only from consumption but also because they stand in no place. The barmaid wants to sell us her house since we find Falls City so interesting. She recommends a bucket of beer which turns out to be 6 bottles of Bud on ice.

The band lights up a solid funk which collides with the vacancy between the walls. Indifference soon becomes resentment. After two from the bucket, I watch the women not hanging on their boyfriends' biceps plough through the lassitude of red Nebraska sweatshirts toward the exit. All the time pg 2 continues to deliver a hard drive from the past. Lotsa horn and rhythm, red hot and cool. And we're moving with it in our booth. Suddenly, the pool chalker yells out, "You're too damned loud." Somebody pulls the plug on light and sound. Biceps hangers moan for attention. Hardly audible, the guitars strum "row, row, row your boat" which leads into a flawless segue of "Old McDonald had a farm ei ei o." The horns walk off stage and blast the chalker's face. It's tense until the chalker backs off like a cold war missile leaving a Cuban harbor. Sound and light return.

In the john a local retching into the toilet tells his buddy at the urinal, he can't remember the last time he felt so depressed. I want to say, "You mean since Columbus Day? That was the big lost game." Pg 2 finish their set and we hit the door. From our hotel window Sharon and I watch them stagger to their pickups. The last to leave is a female and her stalker. Her pace fluctuates between bump and weave. She occasionally looks back to keep track of her stalker. Parked beneath our window she leaves the car door open and he's on her with a three-week passion. Heavy grope until she slaps his hand on her crotch and throws him out. She lights a cigarette, then follows his pickup out of town. "Well, that's the second set to this night," I say. "The genetic pool dried up in this town a long time ago. Couldn't support a tadpole." Sharon reminds me, "It's like Carolyn said, 'beauty and intelligence bust out' leaving only a bunch of mutated frogs."

Another Nickel

for Roy

again reminded
never trust a nickel
the latest dash being Clark's enthusiasm
quoting from his journal
"The Ocean In View" minted
editors disagree
both Thwaittes and DeVoto
disclaim the accuracy of
from where he stood he couldn't view
the ocean, but the salt air from the bay
must have been sweet

Deep Fried

Clouds skid over black ice in the parking lot
I have been assigned the pod with a homogencous
sunflower motif, the cisplatin drips
saline stings the nostrils, decadrone
salt and then steroid with a mouthful of stress
trying to discover a word to lean on
only to lean back into oozal
hooked up to the chemo
cocktail pumped by an infuser
made in Singapore, hearing the voices
with my ear to their lips, remind me
of the ruins at Chacmoltun, but difficult to focus
my mind has always been like a Joseph Cornell assemblage
following a path of marigolds, as the souls do on dias de los muertes
back to their house where there is a beer and a pack of Parliaments
while life is strung from one catscan to the next
only survival is all there is through the fog or storm
on a makeshift stage, to be remembered is unnerving
the Sumerian goat in the tree
has lapis lazuli for eyes, the goat's bar eyes
are vacuous make wild the day
the cocktail continues to drip. We all have our small moments
to remind us of how useless we are
went horseback riding with Joan Baez
the morning after her concert
a tale I have told too many times
when I go as far as I'm concerned you will come
with me into the essential flame, until then I will rail
against the arrogance and disillusion, the remoteness
I have put to a cadence sprung like a jack-in-the-box
to the slow places which otherwise would go unrecorded

Photo by Sharon Moritz, 2006

From either way you go you go to the heart spine joining, the catty cornered artery of the continents, land and life and story, Mayan windows to chemotherapy, the Yucatán Peninsula to the Alexander Archipelago, catfish and gar at the center crossing, the Monkey Scribes to Lord Byron and Meriwether Lewis meeting at the Divide, nowhere else to meet, no more exact than here — "I will rail / against the arrogance and disillusion, the remoteness / I have put to a cadence opening / like a jack-in-the-box / to the slow places which otherwise would go unrecorded" — I would follow all the muddy roads of his obsession everywhere they take, and on beyond, no more willing companion of the ways to have, and this poetry, ever.

~ Kenneth Irby, June 2007

So only to tessellate the social mosaic
two miles north from the trail is a farm
where Mike Ryan gathered his own
with Yahweh's divining arm
he learned from Wickerstom,
the homegrown aryan hate preached by the posse comitatus
soon turned on his own, "Disc the pasture" meant death
the women are mine, Yahweh divined, the weak shall sodomize the goat
the child Ryan kicked, "Disc the pasture" and Dennis Thimin
brought before Ryan's teenage son
Yahweh wants me to skin him with a razor

But we drove south on fresh tar which now connects Rulo
to White Cloud, White Cloud to the Kickapoo casino
followed the river and bluffs winding and the light
so clean between cottonwoods, a river so muddy
changing her course, how to keep her within her banks
how to be other than labeled female, to keep any of us who care
to know the language as other than currency
yes, one hand at black jack, nines doubled down on a Sunday
dealer with seventeen, as sullen as she could be, had to raise
another nine, gas money, bingo in the big room and buffet
Sharon informs me after her reconnaisance
what keeps the parking lot filled with Harleys and SUVs

Sometimes We Eat Salmon

[an interlude from the frenzy]

M/V Kennicott

Bereft, the local replaced by tonnage
the Narrows support
                        cruise ships
five, six a day docked at Ketchikan
watching the spandex disembark, fall prey
to the promoter's hustle, furriers and Swiss gem merchants
tour buses to collect the others
and on the Kennicott as we passed Mud Bight
where we shared a morning calm
with ravens and mosquitos, while the totems
swept across the bow with an idle fix

Nor do these dark hills, cedar and hemlock, seem torn
from Asia anymore with no way back
to simply find a place without making too much
of the serenity in a Chinese scroll
Raven would have torn this landscape
had not Cook and the others with sail
evanesced the old ways

Lassitude before coffee, a blend we travel with
living in my mind for the post-lysergic collage
sometimes a wild gypsy score like sails set to wind
from someplace, say Barcelona, overcomes doubt
but there is chill and mist in my face

A wall of fog eludes us, always just beyond
behind it the souls of dead sailors float
to which our sea monster argues
no, they are not the souls
but my children sprung from those I have killed

Omaha

The drive south on 12th is on an hispanic artery
pumped by the meat packing plants
lots of mom & pop comidas
but we were questing
catfish at the end of the tail

while waiting to be seated
a gar circles a ceramic pond counterclockwise
in fresh water, clear enough to see the coins
tossed for an aimless wish, the gar circles
out of its water which would be the Big Mo sludge

fishermen who snag a gar reeling in their line
take out a vengeance with knife or boot
but this particular gar circles and thrashes
like Dante's fornicators or late Pound
circling Language with one foot nailed to the floor

A Gar's Song

I dedicate this poem which I have retuned
from "Where Rolls the Dark Missouri Down"
to John G. Saxe and Robert Herrick

Industrial river to rail
smelters, grain elevators
beef on the hoof
sky is murky, river too
Old market entrepreneurs
cool antiquarian booksellers
Dodge St for cocktailers
with a view from the roof

"COme down and dance ye in the toyle"

River town, boom town
out of towners, big swindle
treaties written with indian dust
wholesalers, freighters
real estaters, destiny for
manifest lust

"COme down and dance ye in the toyle"

High rollers, claim clubbers
boundary stakers build track
so I sing in jerky style
while they roll one claim to the next
shucking the homestead act

"COme down and dance ye in the toyle"

Big pocket grafters, telegraphers
lawyers, you've been there, right
with the scalpers, lap dancers
so long in this tank, a "Prisoner of Chillon"
hey walleye, don't call me a gar, I'm a pike

"COme down and dance ye in the toyle"

CATFISH FRENZY

CATFISH FRENZY

John Moritz

First Intensity Press
Lawrence, Kansas

Acknowledgment: I wish to thank the editors of the following publications in which some of these poems, often a variation on the present form, first appeared: *Skanky Possum* (Dale Smith and Hoa Nguyen), *First Intensity* (Lee Chapman), *House Organ* (Kenneth Warren), and *Damn The Caesars* (Richard Owens).

Cover drawing: Lee Chapman
Photograph of Davis Memorial: John Gary Brown
Book design: First Intensity Book Arts
www.FirstIntensity.com

First Intensity Press
P.O. Box 665
Lawrence, Kansas 66044

A Riddle

Autumn feels like
a ryderless horse

with the shrill voice
of spring behind

Indian Cave State Park, Neb

                    from where we stand
the mantlerock, the stuff beneath the soil
combines glacial dumpsite and a rain wash mix
with red dust Oklahoma panhandle
this is known as the "Peorian loess"
like the lament in a country tune

    And the leaf state, this mid-October
provides the rush, spreads out across
the Missouri River bottoms north
after the twist from Westport
one ridge to the next
willow to ash, sycamores bleached by a whisper
how many heartbeats left for a scattering of maple
ocher to vermillion between the oak and shag bark domain
offer a brief resplendent but false solitude
little more than poetic leisure, really
I should apologize for the muddy roads
of my obsession taken only for a view
no more than the façade of wilderness
where cables hum beneath our feet

2

Lewis and Clarkers disgorge from the Pillager
"forced to eat dog," etc., the driver recites with a gesture
repeating the documentary
Everyone's imagination buzzes like Musquiters
then the kids split to run and climb
Actually dog was preferred to the Chinookan custom
drying then pulverizing   Salmon   adding sea water
until a salty mush
                    "they gave us to eat some fish and sold us fish,
Wap pa to roots three dogs" [Clark]

*

She knew the way, Sah-cah-gar-we-ah, kidnapped by the Hidatsa
sold to the hands of an abusive Frenchman, she remembered a few
landmarks like street signs along an avenue once traveled another life
so if she was indifferent, no

> ". . . immotion of sorrow . . . or of joy
> . . . restored to her native country" [Lewis]

she had a fondness for tubers
knew where to find them

> "if she has enough to eat and a few
trinkets
> . . . she would be perfectly content
anywhere" [Lewis]

she defined the route by resignation

When Clark took a vote on whether to stay at Cape Disappointment
or go elsewhere
> York sided with Colter for a cove sheltered
from the storm

Janey in favour of a place where there are plenty of potas
> [aka Sah-cah-gar-we-ah]

3

Petroglyphs serve as a magnet for chisel
so many names, some intruding
by those who want their flame etched in stone
the walls are covered with
                              and the petro-quadrupeds
have sprung from a syphoned imagination
not long before the pox

"I with five men . . . assended the Ne-Ma-haw about three Miles
. . . after going to Several Mounds . . . observed artificial Mounds
[or as I may more justly term graves . . ." [Clark]

The park service deemed the chisel a vandal's tool
erected a boardwalk for public view of what is
a dog and pony show

". . . I observed some Indian Marks,   went to the rock
which juiced over . . . and marked my name & date & year" [Clark]

Let them have their chiseled names and heart
should have made a rubbing of dream's abstraction
years ago inside a cave no longer public view

____

PS:
when Byron died so did the marketplace for poetry
who would dare to have their Fletcher
carve his name beneath Byron's on the column at Chillon?

CERTAINLY they would have met on the continental divide. Brooding dark, dark clouds, as if filled with their thoughts, race above them. Byron would be the first to speak.

"These peaks are young like a god's afterthought. The alps have seen Hannibal and his elephants. As I wrote in 'Childe Harold,' I am the rider of the wind, the stirrer of the storm."

Lewis corrects him, "That's not from Harold but Manfred which leads to his staring into the abyss before the Shamas Hunter arrives—stain not our vale with thy guilty blood. I think I quote that true."

They both laugh. Byron paraphrases Dante: "There is no joy in the world can give like that it takes away. I see a fragment of Manfred in you. Walk away from what you think you owe to mankind. You're with the corps of discovery. So you're thirty, and for many that will be half their existence, but you and I will be denied that tottering of age. Forget the guilt, you owe mankind nothing."

"You've read my journal."

"No, it is written on your face."

"My mind dwells on the state of this expedition which I have held in equal estimation of my own existence. I realize I have been unhinged by this desire."

"We use desire too frequently. Meriwether, we have refused the dance."

After some reflection, "Byron, we would have been out of step anyway."

"Your country is young like these peaks. America is vast not only because of the frontier, but also in the passion you have for democracy.

Look at the vote Clark took at Cape Disappoint. Everyone, Clark's slave and Sacahgarweah were entitled their say. Had Shelley lived maybe we would have sailed to America. We discussed it. Alas, I have exchanged my pen for a sword. I'm bound for Greece."

"Yes, Byron, Clark was a wise choice. He was the sweat house healer more than me, but I negotiated the exchange, health for horses. He promised York his freedom, but all that changed when we entered Christy's tavern in St. Louis on the 23rd of September. The equality of the corps was thrown through the roof with our first beer. Clark backed off on his word and refused to sign the writ proclaiming York's freedom. At times I admire Colter for his decision to remain in the mountains."

"I've enjoyed our afternoon, Meriwether."

"Would you like a medal with Jefferson's likeness?"

"No, someday there will be Stuckey's. But I will have Fletcher carve our names and date into a stone."

Catfish Frenzy

1.

Place a whole cat, head to tail
eyes clear and vacant into a bowl full of buttermilk
to purge river from flesh and eggs to bind
let rest before dredging in a cornmeal-flour mixture
add a thrice pinch of salt for salt should always
kiss a fish from any water and be aggressive
with the pepper mill. Holding the tail carefully
ease the cat into an iron skillet with enough lard
hot but not smoking to cover half
fry with patience turning cat when the cornmeal
promises an autumn sunset, then drain on a towel
and serve with a bounty of lemon wedges.

2.

Take a farm-raised by the tail and dip
into eggs beaten like the morning news
recovering   in a bowl   of buttermilk
then dredge in a flour-cornmeal mix
adding salt and an extra Tina Turner shake
from the grinder with a combo of dried
herbs, like thyme, oregano, tarragon etc
drop into the fryer, and recite from
"Prufrock" or "Howl" questioning "dare
to eat a peach" or "I've seen the best minds"
until the cat rises like a harvest moon from
the bottoms, drain on paper towels and serve
with an abundance of lemon wedges.

This photograph of "The Vacant Chair" section of the Davis Memorial was first published in *Soul In The Stone, Cemetery Art from America's Heartland* (University Press of Kansas, 1994) by John Gary Brown. Used with permission.

Davis Memorial, Hiawatha

    catfish gossip

Did she sit in the vacant chair when the first shaft of light
strikes the angels of mourning who reveal the couple on their
                                        [wedding day
finely sculpted marble, Italianate, depicts the passage of how they aged
but no embrace, two birds on a wire, resolve   not grief   keeps them
                                          [there

in chiseled marble, all but the granite, vacant chair
did she stare into the cold eyes of the amputee who outlived his wife
who came from hoarded, disapproving wealth
while he worked the farm, amassed a fortune
all to church, in the catfish diner, though others say family
same as all to the church but burial her will decreed
so this Memorial to keep from rigid protestants

*

where angels kneel now rise take wing and fly toward Baghdad
transmute to turkey vultures, Rumsfeld coined "shock and awe"
from their feeding hiss and grunt, they scan for young liver
beneath the rubble, a mother clutched her child

a pack of crescent hounds tired of rancid grocery meat
gnash at the flesh of a young Alabama boy
one canters across the street wolfing down a large intestine

did she hear Duncan's stutter from the wind
a line not exactly his nor mine, if there was a god
the sod would be torn from the earth, nothing would ever grow

*

let the trees reign, listen to their inflection, pines whisper, maples
                                                        [brag
oaks shout, locusts threaten, willows weep, etc.
sets a paradigm for any journey
the World should live in a poet's mind
and listen to Martha Argerich on the keys expelling demons
from a Shostakovich brooding carnival on the radio to
radials bridging the Nehama for Rulo catfish
crisp as falling leaves

So We Brought Our Own Lemons to Rulo

So we brought our own lemons to Rulo
listening to the librarians behind us talk Lewis and Clark
a show at the Joclyn in Omaha, maps and the promise
maps and liberty, exploration's equality
only to say their journals are so lovely
I hear Clark's determination, Lewis's romantic doubt
Colter's desire to be a mountain man
York denied his freedom, who carried his weight
while presented as a song and dance man
the white world all too familiar
Sioux and Shoshone curious to see a black, women for black cock
Lewis used to make a deal for horses with:

". . . we had a man with us who was black and had short curling hair,
this had excited their curiossity very much. and they seemed quite
anxious to see this monster as they wer[e] the merchandiize we had
to barter for horses" [Lewis]
all the old lies surfaced on the return
St Louis build your arch
Clark's head in a hub of document
reneging on that promise "freedom"
lacks a Captain's signature